THE
TRAVELING
TEAM

The Traveling Team Press (PO Box 567, Conway, AR 72033) functions only as book publisher. As such, the ultimate design, content, editorial accuracy, and views expressed or implied in this work are those of the author.

Unless noted otherwise, all Scriptures quotations are taken from The Holy Bible, English Standard Version® (ESV®), Copyright © 2001 by Crossway, a publishing ministry of Good News Publishers. All rights reserved. ESV® Text Edition: 2016, Italics, bold, or underlined in the biblical text are added by the author for emphasis.

ISBN: 978-0-578-85043-6

In recognition of the time and hard work given by the staff of
The Traveling Team, we would like to thank the following people:

PROJECT MANAGER:
Amber Callison

CONTENT EDITORS:
Todd Ahrend

Caroline Studdard

Molly Johnson

AUTHORS:
Claude Hickman

Seth Foor

Caroline Elksnis

Todd Ahrend

Molly Johnson

Amber Callison

Tanner Callison

Sean Cooper

CONTENTS

101 WAYS TO IMPACT THE WORLD

IS THAT YOUR ONLY ARROW?

The Church has become too dependent on short-term mission trips as its only mobilization strategy. What would you do to mobilize your church or students if there were no trips to take, no flights, no cross-cultural experiences, no crickets to eat, and no souvenirs to bring home?

For many, their entire mobilization strategy falls on taking a series of trips somewhere. Is that the only arrow in our quiver to strike the heart of God's people with His urgent global task? Surely not! Given that Jesus never traveled more than 120 miles from His hometown, I would argue we need to dig a little deeper into what mobilizes people to God's mission in the first place.

Why do we only grab one arrow from the quiver, when God has given us a quiver full of arrows? It comes down to the questions we ask.

IS THAT YOUR ONLY REASON?

No one asks hard questions when you say you want to go on mission with God. I think most assume every action, every motivation, and every expense under the umbrella of global mission is pre-approved by Jesus.

I remember I was on the phone with a mission agency I respect; I asked how my wife and I could take a vision trip to see if we wanted to work long term with Muslims in Central Asia. Sounds pretty good right? However, as the conversation turned to why we wanted to take this special trip it started to sound different.

"Well, to learn more about the city and the people," I said.

"Why couldn't you just read one of the many great books about that city and the work God is doing there?" responded the agency mobilizer.

My next reason, "Well, we want to pray over the city."

"Again, there are great resources like Operation World, Joshua Project, and specific places online you can learn what to pray for that city. The resources will tell you way more than you could discern being there in person for a short-time," she responded.

My third reason never came out of my mouth. As I was thinking about the chance to meet and interact with "real Central-Asian Muslims," God graciously reminded me of the hundreds of "real" Muslim international students who were studying... wait for it...in my own city! Sometimes the Holy Spirit whispers to me – sometimes He uses a sledgehammer. I was so locked into going, I couldn't see the opportunities close to home.

"You know, I guess you are right," I admitted. "The vast majority of what we want to learn and understand could be done right now. I was just being lazy. And a trip sounded more exciting."

We still need to go – 100%. We, at The Traveling Team, are big believers in short-term mission trips and getting people among the nations in person. I believe it is very effective in starting a long-term passion – there is something about going that God uses to grab the hearts of His people. The gospel must be presented to people, primarily through personal relationships and the planting of churches within each people group.

But what do we do when going is limited or not possible? I've met many committed Christians who have real hindrances, real disabilities, real barriers that are not related to sin or fear or disobedience. Sometimes we are limited for a season, and sometimes it is a lifetime. I've had a chance to wrestle through this question and decided that God has valuable Great Commission work for all believers. It may not involve a cross-cultural move, but it will always involve a cross-carrying sacrifice.

The bottleneck is not with God, or a government, or with travel restrictions – the problem might be squarely on us for failing to think outside the box a little. Actually, thinking outside the box should lead us back to the Bible. And in Scripture we find at least four other arrows that God has given the church to mobilize apart from traveling. So, don't throw up your hands and quit. You might just discover your most strategic new mission's ministry has been right under your nose the whole time.

GOD HAS GIVEN US CREATIVE AND EFFECTIVE WAYS TO MOBILIZE EVEN WHEN TRAVEL IS NOT AN OPTION

As advancement in travel becomes more accessible, the advancement of globalization has perhaps made travel less necessary. Paul needed to travel to many places for an initial visit to know how to pray, give, or minister, but that's not true for us. We can now learn about unreached peoples from dozens of reliable mission organizations who have compiled decades of data on hidden peoples and cultures in every corner of the world. We can still pray.

God has planted strategic cross-cultural workers in many areas of the world who are positioned to do ministry in unique ways that we can't. They only need the resources. With only .001% of Christian income going to the unreached – maybe this is an area we could focus on. Directing our resources for better alignment in the unreached through partnering with what God is doing already. We can still give.

Just like the Ethiopian Eunuch in Acts 8, God is bringing the most strategic individuals in the world within miles of our churches. One example is the 1 million international students who are here. America is the most diverse nation in the world where we can find Muslims, Hindus, and Buddhists in almost every suburb in the nation. Opportunities like this are such a strategic crossroads. God moved to interrupt Philip's vibrant ministry in Samaria and sent him to a desert road so that the gospel would return with this influencer to Ethiopia. We have the same strategic opportunity. We can still reach the nations among us.

The Church always needs a prophetic voice to call us back to God's global mission. Mobilization is awakening people to the Biblical story of God reaching all nations, the remaining needs of the world and the Christian's responsibility. None of this requires travel. We have enormous opportunity to plant seeds for a new harvest of global workers. We can still mobilize the Church.

The Traveling Team wants to give you 101 ideas to join in with God and His mission when your travel plans are interrupted. Don't treat the ideas as a check list to mark off, but as a resource to inspire, encourage, and change the way you pray, give, welcome, go and mobilize.

God's mission has not stopped, and neither should we.

01 02 03 04 05 06 07 08 09 10
11 12 13 14 15 16 17 18 19 20
21 22 23 24 25

WAYS TO PRAY

When considering ways to be involved in the Great Commission, prayer would rarely be the first thing on the list unfortunately. When prayer is mentioned as a mission's strategy, there is a good chance we just threw it on there because we knew it was the correct "Bible" answer. In our go-go-go, results-based culture, prayer can feel like a waste of time. Why pray when you can be out there sharing the gospel? Why pray when there are people to be discipled, or churches to plant? Why pray when there are seemingly much more "effective" actions to give our time to?

The answer to these questions is simple. Jesus commands us to pray: "The harvest is plentiful, but the workers are few. Therefore, pray earnestly to the Lord of the harvest to send out workers into his harvest" (Luke 10:2).

When we think we know what strategy or to-do list will reach the most people but forget to pray, we miss the heart of God. When we pray, we show God that we trust He is in control of the Great Commission. He does not want us to work hard on what we think will work; He wants to lead us in what He knows will work and that starts by submitting ourselves in prayer.

For so much of history the "harvest field" Jesus mentions in Luke 10 was ambiguous. Two thousand years ago, Christians could pray for laborers to be sent into the harvest, but they had no idea how massive the "harvest field" truly was. In our modern world, we have access to information on over 17,000 people groups in over 200 countries and there are so many ways to pray for these people and their needs. We can pray specifically for the unreached people of the harvest where there is a good chance, they will never hear the gospel. We can pray for workers to be sent to the least reach people and places around the globe and much more. When we seek the heart of God in prayer and ask for Him to move around the world, we will become an unstoppable force for the Kingdom.

01 Download the "Unreached Of The Day" App.

The Joshua Project is a research organization that focuses on reaching the unreached. They have spent decades researching every unreached people group in the world. The app is one of the easiest ways to expand your vision and passion for unreached peoples. Every day, the "Unreached of the Day" app presents a photo, map, basic statistics, and prayer items for a different unreached people group. At the bottom of the app, it lets you know how many are currently praying with you.

Jeremy downloaded the "Unreached of the Day" app and every week at his Bible study, someone in his group reads the people group profile and they pray for the unreached people group. What an unbelievable tool we have in our pocket with excellent content and prayer points to pray every single day! Scan the QR code to download the app.

02 Stay Informed With Global News.

What happens when you take a look at the news through the lens of the Great Commission? Prayer happens. However, it's hard to pray for the world if you don't know what is going on in the world. Watch the news and pray for the global events God might be using to advance His gospel. "Pray the News" by Missions Network News (MNN) is an incredible resource for staying up to date on global current events. MNN exists to inform multitudes about stories that matter and empower people to take action that changes lives. Each news article gives context of the current event, a profile of the country of origin, and prayer points to help guide you in prayer for the country or event. Subscribe by going to MNNOnline.org or scan the QR code to get the latest news via email.

03 Pray According to Scripture.

During his ministry on earth, Jesus gave his followers specific things to pray. Luke 10:2 says, "And he [Jesus] said to them, "The harvest is plentiful, but the workers are few. Therefore, pray earnestly to the Lord of the harvest to send out workers into his harvest." Is the harvest plentiful? Yes, it grows by 70,000 a day or 26 million a year. Are the workers few? Yes, there is one missionary for every 250,000 in the unreached. Only 3% of missionaries go to the unreached. Indeed, the harvest is plentiful and the workers are few. What does Jesus say in light of this huge need? His answer is simple. Pray to the Lord of the harvest to send out workers. When you pray Luke 10:2 you are praying according to scripture and God will respond.

When you pray according to scripture you are asking God to send out people in your community group, Bible study and church to reach the world. Pray them out by name. Pray for people to go to specific people groups. Pray for your church to send more missionaries than they thought possible.

Nick began to pray the Lord would send out workers into the unreached. After several months of praying, he realized he was the answer to his own prayer! What verses have you read that you could pray as powerful prayers for the unreached? Pray those!

04 Tune Into World Wednesday.

Every Wednesday, The Traveling Team hosts World Prayer Wednesday on our Instagram using the "Unreached of the Day" app. Each week we start an Instagram live event at 10:40am CST and pray for the unreached people group of the day. People can ask to join the Instagram Live and pray alongside The Traveling Team staff. One Wednesday, a girl from Brazil tuned in to pray, and she prayed for a people group in Portuguese. It was such a beautiful picture of the global body of Christ -- worshippers from every tribe, tongue and nation! Scan the QR code to connect with our social media.

05 Commit to Being a Prayer Partner.

When people are sent overseas through a mission agency, most often they are required to raise financial partners. When someone is sent overseas by Christar, a mission organization working amongst the unreached, they are not only required to build a financial team, but also a prayer team. Each missionary must raise 100 prayer partners who will commit to praying for them every day. This is no small task. If you don't know any missionaries, reach out to Christar.org and get connected to one of their missionaries who is looking for faithful prayer partners. Goers can't go if senders don't send. Sending through prayer is an essential role in reaching the world. Use this QR code to become a prayer partner.

06 Set an Alarm for 10:40 or 10:02.

Ellie, a student from Missouri State University, realized that despite her desire to pray faithfully for unreached people, days would go by without even a thought of people without access to the gospel. In light of that, she decided to set an alarm on her phone to go off every day at 10:40 to remind herself of the lost and to pray on their behalf. If the alarm sounded while she was out with friends, Lizzie also had the opportunity to share about the 10/40 window and why she set the alarm in the first place. The alarm served as a reminder to pray and a great conversation starter about God's heart for the world. Another option is to set an alarm for 10:02 in alignment with Luke 10:2 and Jesus' instruction to pray for workers to go into the harvest.

07 Buy Operation World.

Operation World has been one of the greatest tools for prayer mobilization for the world since it was first published in 1974. This longstanding and trusted resource cuts through the fog to provide an up-to-date snap-shot of what God is doing among the nations in the world. Operation World will become one of your most valuable books for understanding the nations and how to pray for them. Joe bought Operation World and began to pray through all the unreached countries. He got hung up on Afghanistan and began to pray daily for the country and as he did, God created a burden in his heart for the people there. Joe would later move to Afghanistan as a missionary and serve there for fourteen years! The decision to move across the world to the unreached started with the choice to pray faithfully through Operation World. Scan this QR to buy your copy.

08 Buy a Map.

Annie and Samantha, students at the University of Central Arkansas, were roommates and both wanted to grow their hearts for the world. As they decorated their college apartment, they decided to hang a huge map on one of the walls with the intent of praying over every country in the world. Each day the girls prayed for a different country and put a tack in it when they finished. Over their junior year, they prayed for every country in the world! Another small group put a map over a dart board and prayed for whatever country they hit with the dart each week. Be creative!

09 Join the Bibleless Peoples Prayer Project With Wycliffe.

Wycliffe is an organization that focuses on Bible translation. They desire to equip and train believers all over the world to translate the Bible for people groups without a Bible in their native language. Over the years, Wycliffe has seen God answer prayers as people pray for specific translation projects to be complete and for unreached people to receive scripture in their "heart language". A five-year-old boy named Sam prayed each Sunday for the Rapa Nui people on Easter Island. One day, Sam heard that Wycliffe had assigned missionaries to work among the Rapa Nui. His parents later discovered that the missionaries had become interested in Easter Island around the same time their son started praying. God is at work through the prayers of His people! Scan the QR to join in the movement.

10 Take a Prayer Walk.

Walk by the international dorms, local mosque, or temples and pray that God would reach the unreached in America who have never heard the gospel. Hana went on weekly prayer walks around her campus praying for international students and asking God for opportunities to befriend them. A few weeks into the semester, she met a student from the Middle East who had never heard the gospel. They quickly became friends and were able to have spiritual conversations. Hana attributes the authenticity of their relationship to God's grace to answer her prayers as she walked her campus.

11 Prayer Points in Sight.

"Out of sight out of mind" is a saying for a reason. It is easy to forget things that we do not intentionally put at the forefront of our minds. Consider putting a laminated Bible verse or prayer points on your mirror, on your fridge or in your car to remind yourself to pray. Alex used a dry erase marker to write a different Bible verse about God's heart for the world on her bathroom mirror each week. Every morning it served as a way for her to memorize the scripture and pray as she got ready. Multitasking at its finest.

12 31-Day Challenge.

If praying for the world is new for you, that's okay. A great place to start is utilizing prayer resources from organizations like "Every Home for Christ." They offer free prayer maps through their website or you can download a digital version.

These maps guide you through a 31-day challenge that helps you pray for the transformation of the nations. By praying every day for a month, you will create the habit of praying for the world.

Each day you are given seven nations to pray for. The map provides you with the total population of the country, the name of the current leader, the percent of Evangelical Christians, and an organization working in that nation. For example, on day 25 you will pray for Botswana, Zimbabwe, Eswatini, Lesotho, South Africa, Mongolia, and China. Mongolia has a population of 3.1 million people and only 1.7% of the country are followers of Jesus. The map prompts you to pray for "open hands, opens doors, open minds, and open hearts".

Scan the QR code to download your free prayer map today!

13 Fast and Pray During Ramadan.

Every year, Muslims participate in a tradition called Ramadan. Ramadan is a month in the Islamic calendar where Muslims from all over the world focus on fasting from sunrise to sunset. During this month, Muslims are spiritually aware and seek closeness with God. It is also a time when many Muslims strive to overcome their spiritual short comings from the other eleven months of the year. As Christians, we have a high value on prayer and fasting, so what would it look like for you to be intentional with prayer and fasting during the month of Ramadan as well? Your reasons will be very different than your Muslims friends, but this could be a great time for you to pray intentionally for your friends and for Muslims around the world.

A good resource we recommend to help you pray during Ramadan is called 30 Days of Prayer. It's a great resource for Christians to pray for the Muslim world during Ramadan. Go to 30DaysPrayer.com to get your resources.

14 Use JoshuaProject.net.

The Joshua Project website is the most complete database of people groups on the internet. They track progress on all unreached people groups around the world. While the "Unreached of the Day" app is a great tool for daily prayer, the Joshua Project website has even more information and data for unreached peoples. They list specific needs and ways to pray for every unreached people group in the world.

The website also includes videos on prayers, resources and articles on how to pray as well as global statistics. They also have several PowerPoint presentations that you can listen to and encourage others to pray for the world. Don't miss this magnificent website that everyone desiring to pray for the world needs to be familiar with. Scan the QR code to access all of the resources mentioned above.

15 Pray for Pastors.

Mobilizing just one person takes a lot of time and prayer. Imagine mobilizing an entire body of believers. We must be praying for our pastors and leaders frequently. Set aside time to pray for the body of Christ you belong to. Pray that your leaders would be faithful to preach mission-focused messages on a regular basis. Pray as they lead, God would grow their hearts for the nations. Pray for fruitful ministry as it pertains to God's mission. An occasional mission's emphasis Sunday can be good, but congregations really pick up on what is emphasized habitually. If God's heart for the world is not something your leadership has vision for, ask God for an opportunity to cast vision for His mission with grace.

16 Intercessory Prayer.

If God answered all your prayers from the last two weeks, would your life look different or would the world look different? How are you stewarding your prayers? As believers, we have the privilege of praying to the God of the universe and interceding on behalf of the nations. Intercessory prayer is the act of intervening on the account of people who don't even know they need prayer.

A man from the Middle East who was living in the U.S., started a ministry that gathered Middle Eastern believers to pray for Muslims around the world. This man overflowed with joy as he recognized his role of intercessory prayer. He prayed for miracles. He prayed that God would reveal Himself to Muslims in dreams. He prayed for Imams to see the truths of the gospel. This man had faith that God would do something radical with the prayers he prayed.

May we have similar faith. May we approach the throne of grace with boldness, believing that God will fulfill His promises and one day we will see people from every tribe, tongue, people, and nation in heaven.

17 Pray in the Car.

Jackson's commute to his campus took him 30 minutes every morning. After he developed a heart for the world, he decided he would use part of his morning commute to pray for the world. Rather than immediately turning on music, he spent the first few minutes of his drive interceding on behalf of people with no access to the gospel. A year later, he began carpooling to campus with his friend Gunnar. Jackson was determined to continue his morning commute prayer time. He invited Gunnar to join in on his daily prayer for the world as well. Gunnar was happy to participate and grew a heart for the world as well through the experience.

18 Journal Your Prayers.

The reality is our minds wander. People tend to feel shame regarding how distracted they get while praying, but rest assured, we have all been there. One way to avoid a wandering mind is to write out your prayers. This will help you stay focused and reflect on the things you talked to God about. There is something special about writing down your prayers. We have met people who keep a prayer log and are constantly writing new requests because they have seen God answer so many of their prayers.

Joe Carter wrote an article for The Gospel Coalition where he referenced there are 650 prayers listed in the Bible and approximately 450 recorded answers to prayer in the Bible. God hears us and he answers our prayers. Get in the habit of writing your prayers and see how God will show up. Scan the QR to check out the article, *"9 Things You Should Know About Prayer"*.

19 Partner With Your Church.

Often, we underestimate the power of prayer. Sending missionaries overseas is not limited to financial sacrifice; the role of prayer is so vital to the health and "success" of ministry overseas. Being a sender isn't "second class," but rather the fuel missionaries need to do the work of God.

One way you can actively send is by reaching out to your church and requesting to receive the monthly ministry updates from overseas workers sent by your church or campus ministry. Read, pray for and respond to their updates. Let them know you are praying for them and ask for specific requests. Be sure to ask your pastor about proper security measures so you don't risk the safety of the missionaries.

Katherine, a student from University of Southern Indiana, gathered a group of friends to pray for the world every Thursday night before their campus ministry meeting. They printed off the ministry updates for missionaries that they knew serving in the 10/40 window and prayed on their behalf. This simple act of prayer has the power to impact eternity.

20 Access the Voice of the Martyrs.

It is easy to take for granted the freedom we have to worship, share the gospel, and gather together as the body of Christ, because not all believers around the world have those liberties. Voice of the Martyrs (VOM) is an organization that serves persecuted Christians around the world. VOM is dedicated to inspiring believers to deepen their commitment to Christ and to fulfill His Great Commission — no matter the cost. Consider downloading the VOM app. You can also request their free Global Prayer Guide, subscribe to the magazine, or even partner in prayer with a front-line worker. All of this can be accessed from their website at Persecution.com.

Jeff and Denise subscribed to the VOM magazine and were both encouraged as they read the testimonies of their Christian brothers and sisters who were persecuted for their faith. The magazine made their family keenly aware that religious freedom is not something to take lightly. They were led to pray for believers whose stories were highlighted in the magazine as well as for the persecuted church at large. Scan this QR code to subscribe to VOM today.

21 Utilize Prayercast.

Prayercast exists to activate victorious, world-changing prayer and worship through mass media and the arts to advance the gospel to the masses. Emily had been praying for Muslims for some time when a friend showed her Prayercast's resources geared towards Muslims. She signed up to receive a weekly email including a video with guided prayer. Prayercast has guided prayer videos for every country in the world. There are over 130 videos for Muslims alone. Emily's prayer life was fueled even further when she read that more Muslims have turned to follow Jesus in the past 15 years than in the previous 1,400 years combined! Visit prayercast.com or scan the QR code.

22 Host an International Food Night.

Neha came from an Indian background and loved to cook meals that were traditional to her culture. During Bible study one week, Neha's friend suggested they all cook a meal together the following week and pray for unreached people in India. The Indian cuisine night was such a hit the ladies made it a monthly ordeal. They chose an unreached part of the world and gave it their best go to cook a meal from that culture. They came to the meal prepared with fun facts about the country, a profile of the country's engagement with the gospel and some general prayer points to pray over as they enjoyed dinner. It was something the ladies looked forward to each month to pray together while growing their heart for the world and enjoying a delicious meal.

23 Pray Without Ceasing.

Scripture tells us to pray always (Ephesians 6:18), rejoice evermore, and to pray without ceasing (1 Thessalonians 5:16-18). These are just a few references that point to having a heart of continual prayer. A practical way you can pray without ceasing is to host a 24-hour prayer event, either virtually or in-person, for the unreached. You can divide up hours for different people to pray or commit to an entire day of focused prayer! One way you can involve your friends or church is by setting up a physical prayer site.

Ethan participated in a 24-hour prayer gathering by signing up for a one-hour shift in a prayer room. His friends set up a prayer room on campus where people came for one hour shifts to pray for the nations. There was worship music and maps on the walls where you could pray over a country. There were also post-it-notes people could write prayers or requests on and display on the wall. A 24-hour prayer time, does not have to be complicated or elaborate, but simply a time to come together and intercede for the nations.

24 Check Your Tag.

Did you know that most of your clothes are made in countries outside of the United States? The top seven largest apparel exporting nations are China, Bangladesh, Vietnam, India, Hong Kong, Turkey, and Indonesia. All these places are packed with unreached people groups. Before you get dressed in the morning, check your clothing tags to see where your clothes were manufactured and pray that the people living there would be able to hear the gospel and put their faith in Jesus. Spencer led a small group during his senior year with a focus on growing hearts for the world. Each week the group began their time together by playing "prayer tag." The guys would check each other's shirt tags and spend some time together praying for the countries that made their shirts – most of which were unreached nations.

25 Pray Like Jesus.

As we read scripture, we see that Jesus was in constant communication with the Father. Not only did Jesus display the value of prayer as he slipped away from the crowds to spend intentional time with God (Luke 5:16), but he also modeled how we should pray.

In Matthew 6:9-13 Jesus says, "Pray then like this: "Our Father in heaven, hallowed be your name. Your kingdom come, your will be done, on earth as it is in heaven. Give us this day our daily bread, and forgive us our debts, as we also have forgiven our debtors. And lead us not into temptation, but deliver us from evil."

If you don't know how to pray, use Matthew 6 as a guide. There are six petitions in this passage that can help us pray: Pray for God to be glorified (hallowed); pray for God's kingdom to come on earth; pray that God would meet your daily needs; pray that God would forgive your sins; pray that he would teach you to forgive others, and pray that God would deliver you from sin and temptation. Our prayer lives should focus on who God is, how he wants us to walk with Him, and what it looks like for God to be made known in the world.

PRAYER IS POWERFUL

As you consider these ideas to expand your prayer for the nations, keep this question in mind:

If all your prayers from the last month were answered, what would look different? Your life or the world?

One day we will be standing before the throne with people from every tribe, tongue and nation worshiping Jesus (Revelation 7:9). Nothing can change this! Jesus has paid for the sins of people from every people group on earth and one day they will stand and worship Him for all eternity. But that reality is some time in the future and right now we get to play a part in getting those people to Christ. Imagine one day in eternity, someone comes up to you and says, "You have no idea who I am. We have never met. But you prayed that God would send a missionary to my people group and He did! And now I am worshiping Jesus with you for all of eternity. Thank you for praying!"

The most effective and impactful thing we can do to reach the nations can be done right now in our homes. Don't sit around waiting to do something. Start praying for the harvest right now and impact eternity!

What does the Bible teach us about praying?

Read the following passages and make observations:

Matthew 9:37-38

Luke 10:2

Matthew 6:9-13

1 Thessalonians 5:16-18

1 John 5:14

Colossians 4:2

James 5:13

Romans 12:2

What is your greatest obstacle to prayer?

_____

_____

_____

Think through all the prayer resources mentioned and pick one prayer resource to start using this month.

_____

_____

_____

Who is one overseas worker you can start praying for consistently?

_____

_____

_____

Who are some friends you could gather (in person or virtual) to pray for the world?

_____

_____

_____

26 27 28 29 30

31 32 33 34 35 36 37 38 39 40

41 42 43 44 45 46 47 48 49 50

WAYS
TO GIVE

Money gives orders. It desires to be our boss. No matter what age we are or stage of life we are in money seeks to control us. This is the point Jesus makes in Matthew 6:24, "No one can serve two masters. Either you will hate the one and love the other, or you will be devoted to the one and despise the other. You cannot serve both God and money." Maybe Jesus spoke about money more than any other topic because He knows its desire is to rule us.

Jesus shares the secret of mastering money: Be generous with it and you will not lack. "Give and it will be given to you. Good measure, pressed down, shaken together, running over, will be put into your lap. For with the measure, you use it will be measured back to you" (Luke 6:38). As God gives to us, we are to then turn and give to others. Your level of generosity toward others is the level of generosity God will have toward you. This principle does not make sense in our economy. In God's economy, it makes perfect sense. The question is do we believe Him?

Being a sacrificial giver is what Christ-followers are called to be. How do we, in this stage of life become a sacrificial and generous giver? Here are some starting points.

26 Make a Budget.

The most strategic thing a person can do to increase their giving capacity is to make a budget. Resources at this age and stage can be limited, but you must be diligent to create healthy habits of spending, saving and investing. Although the idea of budgeting might seem like it could drain the fun out of your life, it is important to have a solid understanding of your overall financial picture. The first step is to talk to your parents. If you receive some financial help from your parents, it is important to understand what expenses, they plan to cover. Next look at your food, clothes, car and entertainment expenses on any given month. As you do, consider categorizing each expense as either a need or a want. For example, most people spend 10% of their budget on food each month. If you think ahead and plan your meals over time you will free up a significant amount of money.

One student at the University of Oklahoma, after he made a budget, was in awe at how much he spent just on entertainment. He made the decision to cut back on movies and even some concerts. That single decision added up to almost $200 a semester! He recognized other areas he could easily cut in order to free up another $40 a month. His next step was to connect with a missionary family and to join their support team for $50 a month. He was only a sophomore! Now he feels a sense of partnership with this family, receives their updates, and prays for them. There's a relationship that comes with the investment. Spending the extra money on himself is no longer a temptation.

No matter how much or how little money you can be flexible with, all finances come from God and it's our responsibility to faithfully and prayerfully steward it. You may have a little now, but someday you will make more money. If the mindset and habit of giving sacrificially are in place, you will transition well to your new financial situation and budget. When you are faithful with little, you will be faithful with much.

For a more detailed list on making a budget as well as a budget spreadsheet, scan the QR code.

27 Get Inspired.

As the saying goes, "Salvation is free, but ministry costs a lot!" Gospel Patrons is a landmark book that will inspire you to increase your giving. It tracks the lives of John Newton, William Tyndale and George Whitefield. Gospel Patrons focuses on the story of how each one had significant donors who invested in them and sacrificed to enable them to change the world. You will be inspired as you read and realize the importance of the giver is no less than the goer! Indeed, behind every great movement of God stands a few generous men and women called 'gospel patrons.' This book invites us to believe God, step out, and serve the purposes of God in our generation. For more on Gospel Patrons, including a list of giving resources, scan the QR code.

28 Buy a Friend a Goat.

It happened to Kyle. In his mailbox on his birthday there was a card from his best friend. He opened it to find his friend had purchased a goat! The card was a thank you from World Vision for the $85 donation made in Kyle's name. The goat was given to a family in Zambia. A healthy dairy goat can give up to 16 cups of milk a day. This simple animal can be a life-changing gift to a family by providing income and a source of food. Giving options range from a chicken starting at a donation of $25 all the way up to a $700 dairy cow. The animals and prices of each are endless. This year instead of a gift card to Starbucks give a gift that could change a family! Scan the QR code for more information on buying a friend a goat.

29 Become a Rainmaker.

Go in to any convenient store and notice how many choices we have in bottled water. From Fiji to Aquafina the choices are endless. This does not even include the water available from the sinks. Now imagine you have no water options. This is the reality for one in three people in the world. Dirty water causes the death of a person every ten seconds. Water For Good seeks to change this statistic.

The average person in Central Africa uses 5 gallons of water per day (compared to the US rate of 100 gallons) which is often gathered from muddy streams and boreholes. Walking miles to collect water full of parasites is absolutely detrimental to people. In order to break the cycle of poverty, you must have access to clean water. Water For Good has drilled and maintained over 1,000 water wells in Central African Republic. Through their Rainmaker Project you can provide clean water to parts of Africa for $30, $60, or $120. Become a part of ending water poverty - scan the QR code to learn more.

30 Take Someone or a Group Through a Study on Giving.

The Church began in Jerusalem and, through the missionary efforts of Paul, spread throughout Europe. Paul loved the believers in Jerusalem and when they needed financial help, he petitioned the church to give. Paul took his third and final missionary journey and travel through Europe pleading with the churches to give a generous financial donation to take back to the church in Jerusalem. This donation was so important to Paul he takes two chapters in the Bible to explain it.

In 2 Corinthians 8-9 Paul tells the wealthy, Corinthian believers how much other less affluent churches throughout Europe had given to the church in Jerusalem. He challenged the Corinthian church to out give the other churches in a donation to the Jerusalem church. Read these two chapters. What do you observe about Paul's passion for giving? What do you observe about what God desires from our giving? Many churches in Europe looked past their need to help others. How can we earnestly share in the privilege of what God is doing globally even in the college years when there is little to offer financially?

Paul challenges us with these words, "The point is this: the one who sows sparingly will also reap sparingly, and the one who sows bountifully will also reap bountifully. Each of you must give as you have made up your mind, not reluctantly or under compulsion, for God loves a cheerful giver. And God is able to provide you with every blessing in abundance, so that by always having enough of everything, you may share abundantly in every good work." - 2 Corinthians 9:6-8

He doesn't say, the wealthy giver or the poor giver. He says the cheerful giver! God rewards the cheerful giver. Your financial status is not a factor to God. Your heart is. Scan the QR code access a bible study guide on giving.

31 Help End Bible Poverty.

The Bible is the most read, sold, stolen and translated book in the world. The New Testament has been translated into 2,256 languages. To put this in perspective, The Adventures of Pinocchio comes in second with 260 translations. Even with all the unbelievable progress there are still 1,713 languages with zero scripture. We call this Bible Poverty.

Ethnos360 is a mission agency founded in 1942 to work among the unreached peoples in the world. Ethnos360 missionaries enter a culture and spend years learning a language so they can translate the scripture for the local people. Once they have translated a certain amount of scripture, they print copies in a bound book to distribute. All this costs money! From start to finish the process to print the New Testament is $277,000 per people group. To break it down even more, each verse is $35 to translate.

Think about what your walk with God would be like if you had no Bible in your language? No way of knowing the truth? No way of knowing Jesus? This is the reality for over 350 million people today. To give toward ending Bible Poverty scan the QR code.

32 Relieve College Debt for Missionaries.

The Go Fund was established for one reason: to relieve college debt for missionaries. The average college student graduates with $29,400 in debt. This is a major obstacle to going overseas. The Go Fund helps to solve the problem. To date The Go Fund is offsetting 71 different missionaries' collegiate debt and has already assumed $3.7 million to pay off! For just $14 a month, you can become a "Ropeholder" and be paired with a missionary going to the unreached. Scan the QR code to learn more about The Go Fund.

33 Give to Pioneers' Relief Fund.

There is so much need right now in the world and it can be confusing and overwhelming to find the place to start. Here is a trusted way to give to the unreached who have been struck the hardest. Pioneers is a mission agency with over 3,000 missionaries on the field working with the unreached. Pioneers and its missionaries are responding with locally organized health efforts. Your gift will help fund projects on the front lines.

One Pioneers family, in a densely populated Asian city, is preparing emergency packets to drop off at homes in their impoverished community. Another Pioneers family is setting up hand-washing stations in front of bus stops in their city. Hundreds of people started using them. The local mosque said, "We've got hundreds of people coming in and out. Can you set one up here?" They ended up having the opportunity to go in the mosque, meet with the leaders, and pray in the name of Jesus with them.

Giving to missions is tied to economic prosperity. When the economy takes a hit, Christian giving takes a hit. The call to biblical generosity is counter to our human nature even at the best of times. Missions is more financially vulnerable than ever. To give to Pioneers' relief fund, scan the QR code.

34 Host a Ramen Holiday.

One bag of Ramen Noodles costs .25 cents. A bag of twenty-four costs $6. Joe was looking at his budget and realized he was spending $40 a month just on Sunday lunches! He then looked around at his friend group and realized it was true of every person. He decided to host a "Ramen Holiday!" What's a Ramen Holiday? Instead of going out to eat, Joe invited people to come eat Ramen at his house for Sunday lunch and charged $10 per meal. He did all the cooking, and all the proceeds went to an overseas worker Joe knew. It was an easy and fun way to get his friends involved in God's mission as senders!

35 Sponsor a Child.

Sponsoring a child with food, schooling, and general well-being, especially a child you have never met, can seem like a huge step. Maybe it is the longer-term commitment or cost that may make you hesitant about even researching this option. Before vetoing this opportunity consider why this may be the perfect way for you to give. Rather than simply donating a sum to an organization, you will be personally connected with the cause. You will receive letters and updates from the child throughout the year and find yourself invested beyond just the money. You will see first-hand health improvements, learning improvements and even spiritual growth.

Right now, through the organization Compassion International there are approximately 260,000 children waiting for a sponsor. Consider what a commitment of $38 a month could do for the future of one child right now!

A college student named Reed stepped out and started to sponsor a child. He says, "I started sponsoring my child when I was 16-years-old. It was the best decision I ever made. Compassion has made a serious difference in her life and is an incredible cause. This organization focuses on every need that these children have: from food stability, to medical, to schooling, and a Christ centered life. I'm now 20-years-old and in college, and no matter how hard my finances can be, I know that I am able to take care of someone else, who needs $38 a lot more than I do." Consider sponsoring a child through Compassion International. To sponsor a child visit compassion.com or scan the QR code.

36 Help End Slavery.

When we think of slavery, we think of history class. Experts have calculated 13-million people were captured and sold as slaves between the 15th and 19th centuries during the Trans-Atlantic Slave Trade. Unfortunately, slavery is not just history. It is very much in our present. And it is more prevalent today than in our past.

Today, 46-million people all over the world are being held as slaves - that's three times more slaves in the world than in the height of slavery in America. Some enslaved people are in bonded labor, while others are held in sex trafficking. Bonded slavery means they are working against their will and under threat, intimidation or coercion. Bonded Slaves produce clothes, make bricks or work in fields. This is most prevalent in Africa, followed by Asia and the Pacific. An example may be a Cambodian villager looking for a better paying job in a neighboring country, only to find himself held in bonded slavery on a fishing boat. Bonded labor accounts for 25-million enslaved people, of which 18% are children. Over four million slaves are sex trafficked, and half of these are children.

Justice Ventures International was started to end slavery! They have developed a comprehensive anti-human trafficking toolkit and advocacy manuals. They rely on lawyers and community members to help those being held in bonded slavery and sex trafficking. To learn more on giving toward ending slavery, scan the QR code.

37 Ask Your Local Church.

Your church desires to see the Gospel spread and you should partner with them in their efforts. Ask the leadership what missionaries have been sent out by your church. Learn about them. Pick one to support. Kennedy did this her sophomore year of college. She asked her pastor if he knew any missionaries who were currently support raising. She was introduced to a couple and is now a part of their monthly giving team and supports the Gospel work they're doing overseas.

38 Be Your Friend's First Donor.

Saying yes to go on a short-term mission's project is the first difficult thing to do. The second is raising funds to get there. Each summer approximately 2.2 million people go on a short-term project. The odds are one of your friends is one of them. What if you reached out to them, expressed appreciation for how God is using them and ask if you can have the privilege of being one of their first supporters. Not only will it exponentially increase their faith, but it will also allow you to receive their updates and pray for them all summer. They will come back changed and you will have played a pivotal part.

39 Create a Social Media Giving Tree.

The average person spends 2 hours and 24 minutes a day on social media. What a fantastic platform to create a "giving tree." Hannah from UC Santa Barbra had a friend who was going on a short-term trip to Central America for spring break and she wanted to help support her friend financially. Hannah decided to create an avenue where more people could join in sending her friend. She chose to utilize social media to post a "giving tree" on her Instagram story. She created an image with a certain number of spots at different giving amounts where people could choose to give. So many of her followers wanted to join in she had to post multiple stories with different "giving trees!" Hannah was able to financially support her friend by using her social media platform and inviting other people to give.

40 Host a Watch Party.

Dylan was a student at Boston University. His friend invited a group over to watch a documentary called "Sheep Amongst Wolves." At first, he thought it would be boring watching a Christian Missionary documentary but felt obligated to go. What he saw completely changed his paradigm. The documentary is about persecution of believers in parts of the Middle East in opposition to the Gospel, and the perseverance of missionaries overcome by the power of the Spirit. Afterward, the friend who had invited Dylan told him about a missionary in the Middle East who is experiencing some of these obstacles! It spurred Dylan to prayer and created a desire for him to give to the missionary. What a powerful visual tool to use to not only increase our faith, but our generosity as well! Scan the QR code to learn more.

41 Put Out a Giving Jar.

During a semester create a giving jar for your small group and pick a mission's project to donate to. Each week you meet have your small group contribute to the jar. Liz did this with her small group, and they were able to collect $300 in one semester! It created momentum each week watching the money in the jar grow. At the end of the semester, they gave the money to one of their friends who was going oversees long-term. It was inspiring for them to see how their money was used to send a friend overseas. The next semester they started a new jar and you can too!

42 Learn a Craft and Give.

McKinley gained a heart for the world, specifically Malawi, Africa while in college. She wanted to raise money and awareness of the Malawi people. She decided to create bracelets to sell to friends and family and then give the proceeds to an orphanage run by missionaries. She learned to create something small that not only raised money for Malawian people, but also helped to grow other's hearts for Malawi. We can support missionaries through simple acts like making braided bracelets. What could you learn to make to multiply funds for others?

43 Join a Campus Ministers Support Team.

Brooks came to Christ through the Cru movement on his campus. He began meeting with the Cru campus minister weekly to further his growth. By his junior year Brooks was leading Bible studies, sharing his faith and discipling other guys. He just was not tithing. He justified not giving by reasoning that his parents were his primary source for income. He could not give. Then Brooks heard a challenging message on giving and decided to start, despite having little income. He thought of a great way to give back to the campus minister discipling him. He decided to join his personal financial support team for $50 a month.

Many campus ministers raise their own salary. What a testimony if you were to come alongside them and say, "As fruit of your ministry and knowing firsthand the impact you have, I would be honored to join your support team." What a partnership as they pour into you, you can give back to them. Consider joining a campus ministers personal support team.

44 Gather a Care Package for a Missionary.

Put together care packages for a missionary that you know. Gather some of their favorite things they do not have access to overseas. Amelia did this for her friend Haley during Christmas. She included snacks that she enjoys and then she added some letters from friends she could open at different points during the year. Haley felt so cared for by this simple act. She knew she was not forgotten. Research a missionary and find out what they miss or just cannot find overseas. Get some friends and gather a care package. It will mean more than you will ever know.

45 Give Your Talents.

We can give more than just money to help support missionaries. We all have gifts and talents God has given us to bless and support missionaries. Graham did this for his friends Thomas and Elizabeth who were missionaries in Asia. During a season of support raising Graham shared how he wanted to support them in a way other than monthly financial support. As a counselor himself, he gifted them with several counseling sessions. He did not know this, but they were in a season where they needed marriage counseling. This was a huge blessing to Thomas and Elizabeth, and they know they will be healthier on the field because of the counseling they received.

How has God gifted you? Maybe it is connecting missionaries with others or a word of encouragement or finding housing when missionaries are home from the field. Maybe it is babysitting the missionaries' children when they are home on furlough or helping with tutoring. We can all give to missions through the giving of our gifts and talents.

46 Ask Your Pastor About Your Church's Global Initiatives.

We can give more than just money to help support missionaries. We all have gifts and Do you love the way your church ministers to people in your community? Then the odds are you will resonate with their ministry initiatives across the world! Many times, we do not realize it, but our churches are often active outside our own communities. Your pastor would love nothing more than for you to ask them for more information on ways to give to their global initiatives and partnerships. Learn what they are doing and join them.

47 Host a Yard-Sale.

We all have clothes and other items we do not wear or use anymore. Go through your closet and find items that you could sell. Recruit your friends to do the same and instead of selling these items on random sites, second-hand stores or simply giving them away, gather the items and host a yard-sale. Invite your friends, family, neighbors, and community to come to the sale and buy the items. Find a specific missionary and give the proceeds of the yard-sale to them. Imagine the impact you could have through recruiting friends who recruit their friends to join you in putting together a yard-sale!

48 Sacrifice Something Each Week

Each month give up a few or more of something you love. Three lattes a month is $15! Loryn was a student at Kansas State University when she was impacted by God's heart for the world. Although she felt like she did not have a lot of money to give, she realized she was spending just under $250 on lattes a semester. She decided to give sacrificially; she would cut out three lattes a week and give that extra money to one of her friends who was going to a summer discipleship project. She did not miss the lattes and her friend appreciated her generosity!

49 Take a Missionary to Lunch.

Buy a meal or coffee for a missionary when they are home on furlough. Evan did just that when one of his missionary friends returned from India for the first time. The missionary got to share his stories of sharing the gospel and spiritual conversations he had with his Hindu friends. Evan asked questions and listened with genuine interest. Spending time and listening are some of the best ways we can love our missionary friends while they are home. Evan also had a chance to learn how he can be praying for his friend well.

50 Design Something.

You can cast vision for giving by designing coffee cups, t-shirts, or stickers to educate or inspire people about the unreached. If people have something they can use, wear or put somewhere it keeps the unreached at the forefront of their minds. They will be reminded of the task still at hand. This is also helpful for people who may not know missionaries personally, but who still want to give!

Maggie is a sophomore with a heart for refugee outreach in her city. She researched and found seven major refugee groups that were located near her. She designed a t-shirt with the phrase "With You," in all seven languages the refugees speak. Not only does this communicate to the refugees that they are not forgotten, but it also mobilized others to join in the refugee outreach and generated funds from the t-shirt sales to put back into the refugee ministry. What would it look like for you to design something that creates momentum and even income to raise awareness for a cause or a missionary?

SENDERS START THE STORY

In Romans 10:13-15 Paul asks four rhetorical questions starting with the unreached person responding to Christ. Paul then works backwards to show the process of this conversion becoming a reality. Paul says, "How then will they call on Him in whom they have not believed? And how are they to believe in Him of whom they have never heard? And how are they to hear without someone preaching? And how are they to preach unless they are sent?"

Look at how Paul flips the script. He says, "How then will they call on Him in whom they have not believed?" The answer is they can't. You must believe before you call.

Then he says, "How are they to believe in Him of whom they have never heard?" Again, the same answer… they can't. You must hear the gospel before you are able to believe the gospel.

Then he asks the third question, "And how are they to hear without someone preaching?" Again, the answer is they cannot. You must have someone change zip codes, learn the culture and language, and preach to them so they can hear.

Now look at the final rhetorical question Paul asks which is the first in the process since he is working backward. Paul asks, "And how are they to preach unless they are sent?" The answer again is a resounding they can't! The one going cannot even get to those who have not heard unless the sender starts the process and gives sacrificially.

Simply put, there is no calling, hearing, believing, or preaching without the sending. Paul says the first domino to be tipped is the sender acting. The sender starts the story. Our generosity starts the story. Our generosity empowers the goer. Philanthropists will be remembered for giving to good causes...you will be remembered for giving to eternal ones.

What does the Bible teach us about giving?

Read the following passages and make observations:

Deuteronomy 15:7-8

Acts 20:35

Proverbs 11:24-25

Proverbs 19:17

Luke 21:1-4

Matthew 6:21

2 Corinthians 9:6-7

Matthew 6:1-4

What is your greatest obstacle to giving?

_____

_____

_____

Think through all 25 ways to give and pick one way you will start giving this month.

_____

_____

_____

Who is one friend or overseas worker who you can start supporting?

_____

_____

_____

If you don't already have a budget, think through how you are spending your money and make a budget. What is one area of your budget you can spend less in so you have margin to give? (Check out point #26)

_____

_____

_____

51 52 53 54 55 56 57 58 59 60
61 62 63 64 65 66 67 68 69 70
71 72 73 74 75

WAYS TO WELCOME

Imagine you're preparing to go to an unfamiliar place. You study the weather of the region, maybe research the most popular types of food or entertainment. You strategically plan out your wardrobe to blend into the crowd or to withstand the different temperatures and weather changes. You realize everyone you'll meet, every place you'll go, and everything you'll see will be out of your comfort zone. Everything you experience will be for the very first time. There is a feeling of excitement and adventure as you arrive and adjust to your new surroundings. But amid this excitement and adventure, you also experience a feeling of being overwhelmed, and even a little anxious. You search for familiar faces but see none. You feel like a stranger.

This scenario is played out every year in the U.S. as hundreds of thousands of international students come to study at American universities. They pack their bags, say goodbye to family and friends, get on a plane and enter a new culture. They come alone and leave any sense of comfort and belongingness behind. They are now strangers in a foreign land. They have become sojourners.

Being a sojourner means more than just being alone in an unfamiliar place. It is also an appeal for help to navigate a new culture, possibly a new language, and even new relationships. As followers of Jesus, we are called to love our neighbors, near and far. We are called to welcome the strangers, the foreigners, and the sojourners. This is made clear in Leviticus 19:34, when God commands, "You shall treat the stranger who sojourns with you as the native among you, and you shall love him as yourself, for you were strangers in the land of Egypt: I am the Lord your God." Just as God provides and cares for us as sojourners in this life, we are also called to embrace international students as sojourners in our country. We see this over and over in scripture (1 Kings 8:41, Deuteronomy 10: 18-19, Ezekiel 24:26-27, Hebrews 13:12). It is a clear command that we can obey and delight in.

God has graciously and sovereignly brought the nations to us and we have the privilege and opportunity to impact the world without ever hopping on an airplane. From sharing meals together to driving them to or from the airport, there are countless ways to welcome international students. We can show the love of Jesus through simple acts that can lead to an eternal impact.

51 Become a "Friendship Partner."

Most international students will never step foot into an American home, let alone make an American friend. As believers, there is incredible opportunity to care for international students. ISI (International Student Inc.) is an organization that exists to bridge the gap between international students and Americans. They recognize most international students are far from home, and often feel lonely and isolated.

ISI can connect you with an international student through their "Friendship Partner" program. ISI paired a family in Southern California with a student from China named Quin. They welcomed Quin into their home, hosted him for dinner, gave him rides, and celebrated holidays together.

This family built a friendship with Quin. He came from a Buddhist background and after spending quality time with Christians, he was interested in studying the Bible. Chase, the dad, met with Quin and two of his Chinese friends to study the Bible together. After months of pursuing discipleship with the students, all three of them accepted Christ and were baptized! International students are hungry for real relationships and searching for spiritual truth. Being in America gives students the freedom from their families to ask hard questions: what is true, what is the purpose of life, and why am I here?

ISI is a great way to meet and welcome international students! Scan the QR code to learn more.

52 Be an RA in the International Dorm.

Living day to day life with internationals in a dorm offers endless opportunities for interesting interactions. From answering questions about odd Americanisms, to helping them learn how to do their own laundry. One of the most surprising gospel opportunities Tanner had in college was when a Japanese student asked him, "What do Americans think about God?"

What if you could live in close proximity to international students like Tanner? Living in close proximity with someone is one of the best ways to build a meaningful relationship.

As an RA you can interact daily with internationals, throw events, and have an excuse to knock on someone's door to check on them. If your campus has an international student dorm, or an area of campus where more international students are housed, you have an amazing opportunity to engage with them by being a genuine friend and sharing the good news of Jesus. It could be one of the most exhilarating and strategic things you do in your college years!

53 Check Out the International Student Office.

Every campus has an international student office where they organize events and activities for international students. This is an easy way to get connected with international students and get to know them in a natural setting. One student visited the international student office and found out they were hosting a cultural potluck in the student union. She was able to attend and befriended a student from South America! From first day of school events to holidays, something is always going on for international students.

54 Check Out Your Campus Ministries International Ministry.

Kate, a student at the University of Colorado, got involved with Cru's international student ministry called Bridges. She was able to connect with a student from Asia named Ming. After a few months of being friends, Kate led Ming to Christ and was able to disciple her for a few months. Ming is now able to go back to her country as a follower of Jesus and take the gospel with her! Ask your campus minister what initiatives they are taking towards international students and get involved.

55 Be an English Language Partner.

Most universities offer what is called, "the language partner program" or something similar. English speaking volunteers assist their international student partners in improving their English skills, help them find their way around campus, adjust to American culture, and become involved in social life on campus.

Zack, from Illinois State University, signed up to be an English language partner on his campus. He felt nervous, because he did not speak any other language other than English, but he wanted to help an international student and also increase his personal ministry. As he walked in to sign up, he had no idea that 118 students from 18 countries were currently looking for partners on campus.

Zack was paired with multiple students from the Middle East. Each week he met with them for an hour to talk so they could practice their English. Through normal conversation he was able to share the message of Jesus, and love them through service, conversations and prayer. Can you find an hour in your schedule each week to serve an international student through conversations like this? If so find out if your campus or community has a "language partner program" or something similar and volunteer.

56 Go Where International Students Gather.

There are certain spots where international students congregate. Whether that is the student union, the library, or the bus stop. Take notice of these places and intentionally spend time there.

Macie was in the public library one day. She noticed a few Muslim women were there too. They were in the children's section reading to their small children. She initiated a conversation with one of them, her name was Hala and she was from Iraq. They became friends and met back in the same spot of the library during the semester. Through their friendship, Macie was able to share the gospel with Hala. Macie was completely astonished when Hala shared that she and her husband had come to Christ, found a church and been baptized! This incredible life impact happened, in part, because Macie decided to go where international students gathered.

57 Download "WhatsApp."

Most of the time, international students will not have an American number. The third-party app, "WhatsApp," is a very popular means of communications for international students. Download and use the app to communicate with internationals even when they go home across the world! Don't let summer breaks be a barrier to communication. Continue to develop a relationship with them over breaks through apps like "WhatsApp."

58 Team up With International Students for Class Projects.

As a senior at Auburn University, Caroline took a financial analytics class where she spent the whole semester working on a group presentation. At the end of the semester each group taught a class based on their group project. She will never forget the day that four international students got up to teach. In broken English, they expressed their apologies and explained they would have loved to work with American students who could have helped them communicate better for the final presentation, but no one wanted to join their group. It was a missed opportunity to show the love of Jesus by both helping and building a friendship with those students. Offer to be in a group with international students or invite them to join your group.

59 Give Rides.

Be available to give international students rides to run errands or take them to and from the airport, because most of them won't have a car! Olivia brought her international friends along with her whenever she went to the grocery store. During the rides, Olivia would share Bible stories and ask them more about their beliefs. She was able to serve them practically and spend intentional time with them. Ask your international friends if they need a ride somewhere or invite them to come along with you. This is a great way to serve them and show the love of Jesus.

60 Join International Student Clubs.

Most universities have International Student Clubs. These clubs include the Muslim Student Association, the Buddhist Student Association and even the Cricket Club where you learn to play the game of cricket. Clubs are open to any student who desires to join and learn more about that particular interest.

Mason joined the Indian Student Association on campus (though he is most definitely not Indian). He was able to meet more Indian students and learn about their culture. After a few years of involvement, the Indian students elected him to be Vice President because they loved his commitment so much! See what clubs are on your campus and join one to meet more students and learn about their culture.

61 Bring an International Student Home.

Often international students won't go home for short breaks because of the distance. School breaks are an incredible time for you to invite internationals to spend holidays with your family. Many cultures place a high value on hospitality, so this is a unique way to love them through welcoming them into your home. You will also be able to introduce them to American cultural traditions, which is usually high on an international students' value system.

During his senior year at Ohio University, Robby invited several international students from his floor to come home with him for Thanksgiving. He ended up taking a Japanese student home with him to spend the break with his family. He enjoyed it! And what's even crazier is his parents loved it, too. They enjoyed it so much they invited his friend to come back and stay with them for a month over Christmas break. And then he stayed over spring break… and Easter! The family became the student's American home away from home. Robby and his family were able to share the gospel with him several times, and a few years later, he actually came to know Christ! It all started with spending a holiday with an American family.

62 Research Your International Friend's Home Country.

Most international students will keep up with what is going on at home. You can keep up with current events as well! A great resource to do this is online at the CIA world fact book. You can also regularly catch international headlines in the news or online articles. Try to pay close attention to countries your friends are from. Not only is this a great conversation starter, they will also be impressed! Scan the QR code to reseach countires around the world.

63 Memorize Verses About God Reaching the Nations.

How can we view the nations the way God does? One way is to memorize and meditate on scripture. What would it look like if the next time you see an international on campus or in your community you were able to pray a verse you have just memorized to become a reality in their life. It could be as simple as "Lord, Psalm 67:1-2 says, 'You God have been gracious to us and bless us and cause your face to shine upon us, that your ways may be known on earth, your salvation among all nations.' Thank you for extending your grace to me and blessing me with knowing you, now I pray you would give me a way to share this good news with Zara the next time we meet."

There are so many passages of scripture that show God's heart for the nations and the futility of the false gods they worship now. Through memorizing verses your ability to pray specific passages for your international friends will began to take on a new dynamic. "Father, Jeremiah 16:19 says the nations will come from the ends of the earth and say, 'Our fathers possessed nothing but false gods, worthless idols that did them no good.' I pray for my Hindu friend Darsh that he would see the gods he now worships are worthless idols. They do him no good. But you alone offer life. Allow me the privilege of seeing him become a follower of you."

Writing scripture on your heart will not only help you align your heart with God's, but also develop a heart for all peoples.

64 Cook a Meal With Your International Friend.

Ask them to make you their favorite dish from home. Molly invited her friend Sam over to make her favorite Egyptian dish one night. Molly was able to engage in conversation with Sam and learn to cook a new meal. It was a fun way to show interest and take time to learn something about Sam's home and culture. You could even teach them one of your favorite American dishes. If you don't have access to a kitchen, ask your friend to take you to a restaurant in town they think does the best job at making cuisine from their home country. Pro tip: let them order for you! They know what they're doing.

65 Grab Coffee or Tea.

Coffee and tea are a universal love language. Use that to your advantage! Many cultures place an emphasis on drinking tea or coffee during social gatherings. This will be familiar to them and something they can enjoy. Moriah wanted to engage with her international friends in a way that would be familiar and comfortable. She knew her friend from the Middle East enjoyed drinking coffee so, she invited her friend to grab some at a local shop. While drinking coffee together, they were able to deepen their friendship and engage in spiritual conversation! Invite your friends over to your house for coffee or tea, or invite them to go to a local coffee or tea shop with you.

66 Sit Next to International Students in Class.

It's so simple, but such a great step to build relationships with your international student classmates. Ben walked into his English class and immediately spotted an international student sitting alone. Instead of choosing to sit with his friends, he went over and sat with him. This was the start of their friendship that lasted all four years of college! Be aware of who is in your class and be intentional of where you sit, because you never know what friendships can come from this small act.

67 Learn Key Phrases.

Language speaks to the heart. When you address someone in their native language, there is an instant link. They will first be shocked that you knew a phrase, and then be honored you would learn it for them. Start with learning to say "Hello" in a few languages then add to your vocabulary.

Here is a list to start with: Chinese (Nee Haow); Arabic (Mar ha baan); Hindi (Namaste); Japanese (Kon nichi wa).

You can ask your international friends to teach you a few more short phrases and take time to develop a small vocabulary in their language. The point of this is not fluency, but connection. This is not only a fun way to engage with them and their culture, but it will show them that you are interested and invested in them. To learn starting phrases in other languages, scan the QR code to visit RosettaStone.com.

68 Host an Event and Invite Your International Friends.

Most of the time, international students might not celebrate the holidays in America. This is a great opportunity for you to host a Friendsgiving, Halloween party, Christmas party, or cultural potluck. It is a fun way you can celebrate the holidays together and teach them some American traditions. You can invite some of your friends and they can invite their friends. During a fall semester, Lydia, hosted a bonfire and students from India, Japan, Saudi Arabia and South Korea came! Imagine how loved and welcomed your international friends would feel if you hosted an event like this for them.

69 Utilize the "Welcoming Internationals Playbook".

The Traveling Team created a resource called "Welcoming Internationals Playbook". This is an incredible tool where you can learn more about different religions, how to engage different people in spiritual conversations, and even find Bible studies to lead your international friends through. You can utilize the tools and articles on this page to help guide you in your relationship with international students. To learn more, scan the QR code.

70 Take Part in International Neighborhood Network.

Every year, thousands of internationals move to America. They are moving from the very countries where missionaries are taking the gospel! Many unreached people are in our very own neighborhoods and communities. World Team recognized this and started an International Neighborhood Network (INN) where you can take part in reaching foreigners in various cities around the U.S. There are a multitude of opportunities to use your skills to reach internationals in our own communities. Scan the QR code to see how you can get involved with INN.

71 Buy a Bible in Their Native Language.

If there is a Bible in your international friends' language, buy it for them and ask them to read it with you. As you read your Bible, they can read along with you in their native language. Reading scripture in the language they are most fluent in will be incredibly powerful. Scripture is living and active in any language, but it will resonate with them the most in their heart language. Don't underestimate how God can use His word in someone's native language to do incredible things!

One church decided to give a young Chinese college student a Bible in Mandarin to take back to his family in China. When he got to China, he gave the Bible to his mom and told her that it was God's Word. She asked him what it said, and he was able to share the gospel with her—and she came to Christ! Then she led her sister to Christ, and they went and talked to their parents, and they came to Christ! After a while, his dad finally came to Christ, too. The spark for it all was that Bible in Mandarin a church gave to an international student.

72 Visit Other Places of Worship.

See if your town has any mosques, temples or other places of worship you can visit. You can meet people and be a learner through asking questions. An international student asked Will, a student at the University of Maryland, to go to the local mosque with him during Ramadan. Will sat in the back and was able to observe and pray for the people during the service. Afterwards he engaged with the people and asked them questions about what they believed. The people at the mosque felt honored to have him and his friend was even more open to spiritual conversations because he knew Will was willing to listen and love him!

73 Eat Ethnic.

How many restaurants are there in your town you have not been to? How many of those restaurants are Middle Eastern, Chinese, Vietnamese, or Thai? Most towns have businesses and restaurants that are owned by internationals, and, many times, international students will frequent these restaurants. These businesses are great places to meet international students and the owners—they're also great places to get tasty food. Next time you and your friends are looking for somewhere to eat, opt for the restaurant you always drive past and never go to. You may meet a new friend and begin a new ministry.

74 Be a Good Host.

Two girls from the University of Texas took a group of international students to a trampoline park. The students had never experienced anything like it and it quickly became their favorite experience of the year. On another campus a student sat with a group of internationals and explained the rules of football. Later in the semester, he took them to the game on campus. They joined in the with the crowd to cheer on the team, because they finally understood how the game was played. Another student took a Jordanian student golfing. His highlight was driving the golf cart. On one of the holes, he even called his family back home to tell them he made a put!

Invite internationals to do fun things. They may or may not have similar activities at home but it will be a whole new cultural experience doing it with you in America. Not only are they experiencing new things, but they are creating memories with you that will last a lifetime!

75 Engage in Gospel Conversations.

Outside of western culture, people are very open to talking about spirituality and what they believe. Many internationals are actually interested in learning about Christianity, because it is widely associated with America. Just like it says in Acts 28:31, "He proclaimed the kingdom of God and taught about the Lord Jesus Christ with all boldness and without hindrance."

Here is a great way to get started. Meet with a Muslim or a Chinese friend and ask them questions about God. Have the gospel printed in their language and ask them to translate it for you. It will lead to an unbelievable conversation.

We can have confidence through the Holy Spirit to share boldly the gospel. Your international friends four years in college might be their only opportunity to hear the gospel. Don't miss out on this opportunity!

Download the app, GodTools, to learn how to share the Gospel in Arabic or Chinese. It is an incredible resource that will help you share the Gospel in a clear and easy way.

WELCOMING MAKES A WAY

These are all things that you can do right now! Each one of us has a role and responsibility to play in reaching the nations, and welcoming is a significant and strategic way to do this. We can actively help to see the Great Commission fulfilled through loving our international friends. Ultimately, our motivation to welcome is love. Simply put, welcoming internationals is a by-product of loving Jesus. When we love Jesus, we are to love His people. And if we love His people, then we will love international students from all over the world. We can make room at our tables and in our lives for these people. We do this not only because Jesus commands us to, but because we love Him.

Most international students will go back to their home country where they may never hear the name of Jesus again. Their four or so years of studying in America, where they have an abundance of access to the gospel, might be their only opportunity to hear the good news of Jesus. Imagine the ripple effect if an international student came to know Jesus in college and took the gospel back to their unreached people. Let's not miss this opportunity! We can be strategic and have an eternal impact on the world tomorrow by welcoming international students on campus today.

What does the Bible teach us about welcoming?

Read the following passages and make observations:

Deuteronomy 10:19

Leviticus 19:34

Exodus 23:9

Deuteronomy 27:19

Zechariah 7:9-10

Luke 10:27

Romans 12:13

Hebrews 13:1-2

Ephesians 2:19

What is your greatest obstacle to welcoming?

_____

_____

_____

Think through all 25 ways to welcome and pick one way you will start welcoming this month.

_____

_____

_____

Research your city to find the local international student ministries and English language centers. Write down one organization you will reach out to about local opportunities. When will you reach out to them?

_____

_____

_____

Can you think of a missed opportunity where you could have welcomed internationals but didn't take the step? What can you do differently if you have the opportunity again?

_____

_____

_____

76 77 78 79 80

81 82 83 84 85 86 87 88 89 90

91 92 93 94 95 96 97 98 99

100

WAYS TO MOBILIZE

If you are taking the time to read this resource, you are most likely a World Christian, someone who understands that God has a heart for the world and someone who desires to play a part. We want to celebrate that, but we also want to encourage you to go a step further and consider the role that you could play as a mobilizer.

You were mobilized by someone to understand both the gospel and the importance of God's mission in your daily life — and now it is your turn to mobilize others! A mobilizer is someone who has a passion for the world and a passion to pass it on. Mobilization is coming alongside the work of God in someone's life to transform their heart towards the things of God's heart. If we desire to finish the Great Commission and see Jesus worshipped among every tribe, tongue, people, and nation, then mobilization must happen.

Below you will see practical next steps you can follow to help others join in on God's mission.

76 Mobilize Others With a Single Sheet of Paper.

What if you could put everything you have learned about missions on a piece of paper with three stick figures, nine lines and fifteen words? The Traveling Team developed a tool called the World Vision Illustration that will accomplish just that! The World Vision Illustration is a reproduceable tool that provides people with a simple and effective way to share what they have learned about God's heart for the world with their friends.

This illustration has equipped thousands of college students across the United States to mobilize their friends. Megan was a student from Kutztown University in Pennsylvania when she heard The Traveling Team share about God's heart for the world and the 10/40 window for the first time. It was then she learned the World Vision Illustration. She had a specific friend in mind with whom she wanted to share the illustration. The Traveling Team knows for certain that Megan shared with this friend because this friend reached out to us to thank us for equipping Megan to equip her. Mobilization multiplies!

The World Vision Illustration is one of the most valuable tools that you can have in your toolbelt as a mobilizer. Scan the QR code for a step-by-step video of The World Vision Illustration.

77 Develop a World Christian Testimony.

Everyone has a story to tell, but not everyone can tell their story well. If you have a heart for the world, there is a reason, and a story behind the reasons. To tell your story, you need to prepare the story. Take some time to think through three things: 1) Your story of becoming a Christian—your story of coming to Christ should be the most important thing about you. 2) When you first heard about God's heart for the world. 3) the impact that God's heart for the world had on your Christian walk.

Once you have answered these three questions, develop a 90 second World Christian Testimony. It is your "elevator pitch" to share with other Christians about God's heart for the world. The reason we challenge you to make a 90 second testimony is because you can always make a short story long, but it is difficult to make a long story short.

78 Watch MomentumYes.

Talking with your friends about missions can be difficult at times. Don't you just wish there was a video (or a video series) that explained everything you wanted to communicate? Well, there is! It is called MomentumYes. MomentumYes is a free online video series that teaches, inspires, and equips everyday people to rethink their lives in light of God's mission. It is designed to actively engage believers in taking next steps to be involved in missions.

Maybe you don't feel equipped to help your friends grow, so grab a group of friends, watch the MomentumYes video series and lead a time of discussion on personal takeaways. Visit MomentumYes.com to start your journey. Scan the QR code to learn more.

79 Organize World Prayer.

Prayer is a wonderful way to mobilize the people around you. Of course, you can pray alone, but organizing a group to pray is a simple way to model a heart for God and a heart for the world. As a senior in college, Jake had a heart for God, a heart for his dorm, and a heart for the world. Jake wanted to be strategic with the guys in his dorm, so he gathered all the believers pray every Tuesday. Their routine was simple: they would pray for each other, pray for the dorm, and pray for the world. For some of the guys, it was odd to pray for each other so regularly, and for many it was new to pray for different countries around the globe. God was faithful through this prayer group. God answered prayers for the guys, prayers for the dorm, and prayers for the world.

80 Use Your Work as a Catalyst.

One of the best ways to mobilize those around you is to incorporate the world into your work, passions, and giftings. Brian started a leather products company called @1040_ leather to raise awareness for the unreached. Referencing the 10/40 Window in the name of his company, sparked curiosity in his customers. It opened the door for Brian to share about the needs of the world and why he cares enough to build a business on the vision of the unreached. What are you passionate about and how can you use it to share God's heart for the world with others?

81 Recruit Your Friends to Go.

Just because you cannot go overseas this summer, doesn't mean that you can't tell your friends to go! Some of your friends are eager to spend time overseas but they don't have the connections to know where to find opportunities. What if you learned about mission agencies and specific trips to recruit your friends to. This is what Dustin did.

Dustin, a student at Western Michigan University, learned about an organization called Trans World Radio (TWR) that offered mechanical engineering internships overseas. He was so pumped that there was such a unique opportunity for mechanical engineering. Dylan was not sure if he was going to be able to take this internship, but he wanted to pass the information on to others.

He shared about TWR with his friend Connor, who was also studying mechanical engineering. Connor was even more excited about the opportunity that he took the initiative and reached out to TWR. He applied to spend his summer in West Africa serving with TWR as a mechanical engineering intern. Dustin, through this simple act, was a mobilizer. Learn about mission opportunities to recruit your friends to, scan the QR code.

82 Host a Mobilization Bible Study.

What if you spent a few weeks during a semester and focused on how God wants to use His people to reach the ends of the earth? There are several Bible studies already developed to help in your quest to cast vision to others. For a fantastic five-week study, start with *Getting a God Centered Cause For Your Life* by Cliff Lea. This is an incredible introduction to the Biblical Basis of Missions. There is also a leader's guide you can download to accompany the study.

If you want to start with a one-week overview the prep has already been done for you. Check out The Traveling Team's study that journeys through scripture from Genesis to Revelation. There are fifteen questions you can ask your group as they read key passages.

Phoebe gathered a small group to go through a mission's Bible study on her campus. She not only took people through the Bible, but she also challenged them to meet one international student during the course of the study. Each week students would share what God did through their encounters with international students. Phoebe even researched to find a local Mosque, Buddhist, and Hindu temple for her group to visit in their community. What would it look like for you to host a mobilization Bible study? Scan the QR code to access the bible studies mentioned above.

83 Read The Ten Modules.

Reaching the world with the gospel of Christ is possible. God has given the church all the manpower and money it needs, a thousand times over, to finish God's global mission. So reaching the world is not a resource problem, it is a mobilization problem. The Ten Modules: Equipping You to Mobilize is a resource The Traveling Team has developed to help you become a master mission's mobilizer. Each of the ten modules builds on the other and offers practical advice on taking someone from onlooker to someone who is invested and involved. Whether you use this in a one-on-one setting or in a small group you will be equipped to challenge others with how God wants to use their time, talents and abilities to reach the world.

From handling excuses, to implementing mission's vision in your group, and even sharing practical illustrations to help others gain a heart for the world, The Ten Modules packs a powerful punch. Author and speaker David Platt says, "I distinctly remember when I first read The Ten Modules and God gripped my heart with His passion for His glory in all nations through it. I praise God for its influence on my life." Scan the QR code to purchase The Ten Modules.

84 Share the Biblical Basis of Missions.

At the end of the day, if anything is going to mobilize people, it is going to be God's Word. Scripture has a far longer shelf life than any cool story or compelling statistic. Marc, a student at Rutgers University, heard The Traveling Team teach on the Biblical Basis of Missions on his campus. After hearing the talk, he was challenged to grow his heart for the world and wanted to help others do the same. He was given the opportunity to share the Biblical Basis of Missions in front of his church congregation. Marc shared from Genesis to Revelation, tracing the theme that all throughout scripture God has a heart for the world.

You might be thinking, "I can't do that: I'm an introvert. I am inadequate. I am not theologically trained. I'm not a public speaker" ... neither was Marc. You know what Marc was? Obedient.

He saw an opportunity to mobilize his church, and he took it.

Understanding the story of scripture is vital for followers of Jesus. This is one of the most important ways you can influence those around you. If you have heard this message, we want to challenge you to share it with others. Scan the QR code to read the article "Genesis to Revelation: God's Heart for the World".

85 Start a Mobilization Club With Friends.

There was a group of eight students from the University of Arkansas who had varying levels of mission's knowledge and experience. They decided to start a mobilization club called 937. At their first meeting they had 50 students gather to hear the Biblical Basis of Missions. They met once a month and brought in different teachers to equip students to be on mission.

One of the founding students said, "the mobilization group called 937 is modeled after the verse, Matthew 9:37. It states, 'The harvest is plentiful, but the workers are few. Therefore, pray earnestly to the Lord of the harvest to send out laborers into his harvest.' This past school year we met every Sunday night to pray for an unreached people group that has not had the opportunity to hear the gospel and for believers to go into the "harvest" to share Christ. Through 937, I experienced a deeper desire to share the gospel with others, to be friends with international students, and to see the unreached people groups around the world come to know Christ! I believe that learning about being a "World Christian" has changed my main purpose and values in college and now post-graduation."

Maybe you can consider starting something similar on your campus or in your church.

86 Explore the World in Your Backyard.

As you saw in the welcoming section, the nations are here! But it can be so easy to overlook what is in our own backyard. This is not your problem alone, your friends, family, and church do not notice what is in their backyard either. Most people do not realize that in most cities, there are temples representing the major world religions, international markets, international restaurants, and entire neighborhoods filled with people from the ends of the earth. One way to mobilize your friends, family, and church is to model for them what it looks like to engage the world around them.

Go to these temples, places of worship, restaurants, and neighborhoods. Get yourself around people with diverse backgrounds who do not know Jesus. But do not go alone! Take your friends to explore and engage with you. Two students from Eastern Kentucky University, Cameron, and Katie, noticed there was a mosque in their small college town. They wanted their friends to understand more of God's heart for all people, so they took their friends with them to engage with the Muslims that live in their city.

What is in your backyard that you can take advantage of today?

87 Lead an Xplore Study.

Holly, a senior at Purdue University, invited members of her campus ministry to a Bible study that focused on the world. Three freshman girls signed up. She spent intentional time with the girls and walked them through an Xplore study. The Xplore study is a seven-lesson study exploring God's word, world, and work. It is a phenomenal resource to help you walk your friends through God's heart for the nations, the needs of the world, and how they can engage today, tomorrow, and for the rest of their lives. Scan the QR code to find resources to start an Xplore study.

88 Memorize Scripture

Scripture tells us to hide God's word on our hearts. What better words to hide in our hearts than words that so clearly display the heart of God? Scripture memory is a discipline that many believers neglect. Often it can be challenging to memorize scripture alone. A powerful way to mobilize people you are in discipleship relationships with is to memorize scripture together. There are over 1,500 verses that reference God's heart for all peoples, nations, earth. Choose a few key verses such as Genesis 12:1-3, Psalm 67:1-2, Matthew 28:18-20, Acts 1:8, and Revelation 7:9 and start memorizing! Once you memorize these verses, check out the article "Genesis to Revelation: God's Heart for the World" at TheTravelingTeam.org and find more verses to memorize.

89 Utilize The Traveling Team's Website.

How many restaurants are there in your town you have not been to? How many of those

The Traveling Team has been stirring university students all over the country to rise up and join God in reaching the world for Christ for over two decades. Think of us as a mission's conference on wheels. During this time, we have gathered the top articles, statistics, and mobilization resources. The Traveling Team's website has become the first stop for every mission's enthusiast who wants to find resources to fuel their vision.

The Traveling Team offers a vast amount of high-quality mission's content ranging from "How Do I Know If I am Called?" to "How Do I Know Who to Date?" Articles with detailed statistics and biblically based content for going and sending. If you have a question about mission's The Traveling Team most likely has an article or resource to help you.

We provide resources for free to help you, your friends, and your church learn more and to help mobilize those around you. Visit TheTravelingTeam.org/Resources.

90 Schedule a Mission's Conference for Your Church.

Each year, The Traveling Team has 250 campus ministry meetings across the U.S., but we also speak at churches. Several of our staff invest much of their time mobilizing churches. You can help make this happen! Talk to your mission's pastor, head pastor, or someone in leadership at your church to explore the idea of having a "Mission Revolution" conference at your church. We offer a customizable conference experience to meet the needs of your church. Scan the QR code to find out how to host a "Mission Revolution" conference.

91 Gather Friends to Watch "Going Global".

Have you ever wanted to learn what it really takes to go to the nations? Or what it really takes to plant a church? Or what it takes to reach the unreached? Have you ever wanted to see principles of the Book of Acts applied to missions today? Then you should gather a group of friends, or a church group, and go through the "Going Global" series by Access Truth. This 10-week series includes a dynamic retelling of the early Church through the book of Acts. It highlights God's global purposes, sketches a realistic picture of the challenges to spreading the good news, and it challenges you to seriously consider how God would have you engage in His mission. Scan the QR code to learn more.

92 Take Perspectives and Invite a Friend.

Grant and Kaylee took a class called Perspectives on the World Christian Movement which trained them in the biblical, historical, cultural, and strategic aspects of missions. Perspectives is a 15-week course offered at churches around the U.S., and online. This class not only rocked their world and their understanding of God, but it also helped them see how impactful it could be for others. So, what did they do? They did not just tell friends to watch the online course, they decided to facilitate and lead their own Perspectives course! They did not have to be experts on all the topics, but they did have to be committed to recruit friends, churches, and strangers, to join this 15-week class that impacted their lives. Their mobilization efforts have helped so many people in their city begin to think about God's mission strategically. To find a Perspectives class near you, scan the QR code.

93 Learn From Your Mission's Pastor.

Mobilizing within your church is one of the most strategic things you can do. A great place to start is to meet with your mission's pastor and familiarize yourself with your church mission's strategy and goals. Ask good questions and ask how you can serve.

Your church might not have a mission's pastor, in that case aim to meet with your head pastor and ask him about the church's mission strategy. This meeting should not be a time for you to tell him everything you learned about missions and how the church could do better. No, not at all. This meeting is a time to ask good questions. Your goal should be to listen well, to share your passion, and to ask how you can serve. Good mobilization is not brash, rude, or arrogant. Good mobilization is loving, patient, and willing to serve wherever there is a need.

94 Be the First.

It can be intimidating to share your faith with someone who looks like you, talks like you and has a name you can pronounce on the first try. Now try it with someone who has none of those three. The sad reality is the average Christ follower does not have any friends from other countries. The number one reason is the Christ follower must take the first step. The international student rarely will. This can be difficult. Someone must go first and the odds are, it's up to you. Step out, initiate conversations and see what friendships God brings in your life with those from other nations.

Jacob was a senior at the University of Toledo when he realized that his campus ministry was the largest on campus, but there were no international students engaged with the members of his ministry. The problem was not that they did not have international students on campus, the problem was many chose not to interact with them. Jacob decided to go first. He began meeting internationals, taking others with him and built friendships that led to gospel opportunities. Now, each semester Jacob leads a group of friends to do intentional outreach on his campus! Jacob was first but now many have followed.

95 Follow The Traveling Team on Social Media.

As an organization, we desire to use our social media to share some of the best mission's content. We know that there are a lot of voices on social media telling you how and where to invest your life, and The Traveling Team wants to be one of those voices. We want to remind you of the goodness of God in Christ Jesus and how His goodness needs to be shared to the ends of the earth! We want you to be challenged and inspired, and we want you to use your influence on social media to share about God's global heart. Like, repost, retweet, and tag us @TheTravelingTeam on Instagram, Twitter, and Facebook.

96 Strategic Stickers.

Do you like stickers? Yes, most people do. People often ask, "what's that sticker from?" or "what's the purpose behind that sticker?" Stickers can mobilize! The Traveling Team gives away free stickers of the 10/40 Window when we travel. We have heard countless stories of students who have put the sticker on their water bottle or laptop, and it has started an incredible conversation with friends, family, classmates, believers, and non-believers alike.

The Traveling Team has a special 3-pack of stickers for you. Stick them somewhere prominent and use them to tell your friends about God's heart for all nations.

Stephanie, from Carroll College, received this 3-pack of stickers and immediately placed one of the 10/40 window on her laptop. She knew that this would be a strategic location to place her sticker where it would not only remind her of Gods global mission, but spark conversations with her peers. She saw this as a unique opportunity to share about God's heart for the world and mobilize her peers when they asked about her sticker. Where could you put your sticker that would spark conversations? Scan the QR Code to sign up to receive free stickers.

97 Invite Others to Go.

Mission Statesman and Noble Prize winner John Mott would always challenge the audience of mission enthusiasts to do one thing... invite their friends! During his nearly 40-years of mission's mobilization, he would remind students that most Christ followers are not interested in missions because no one has invited them to be interested. Mott says, "Thousands of well qualified young men and young women are not even thinking of the missionary enterprise, simply because it has never been brought before them in such a way as to suggest that they could engage in it if they so desired."

Don't just think about what you should do this summer. Invite your friends to join you. You saying "yes" to going overseas and leading the way will actually clear the way for others to say "yes" behind you. We must have a "who can I take with me" perspective.

One young couple had a desire to go to the unreached in Papua New Guinea. They invited two other couples to join them.

One young couple had a desire to go to the unreached in the Middle East. They invited another couple to join them.

One university student desired to go short term to Indonesia. She invited two other students to go with her.

They all said yes! Many Christ-followers are simply waiting to be invited. God is moving them to step out and if you say, "Go with me" it might be the last little nudge they need. Who can you invite to join you in God's mission today? They just might say yes!

98 Become a Mobilization Expert.

Vision leaks. Starting a library of excellent missions' books is a perfect way to keep your world vision fresh and learn from some of the leaders in missions today. The Traveling Team has gathered a list of the top twenty-five books every mission mobilizer needs to read. Here are a few on the top twenty-five:

The Abrahamic Revolution by Todd Ahrend. Understand the missional theme of God's Word, the task remaining in God's world, and our calling to God's work. God's purpose is one continuous and all-encompassing movement to redeem people from every tribe, tongue and nation. You are invited to join the legacy that began with Abraham and will end in God's global glory.

Live Life On Purpose by Claude Hickman. The aim of God's entire Biblical story has one mission, reaching all the nations, and one method by which to achieve it: all believers. Finding your life purpose only makes sense in the context of God's plan to reach the world. Discover the part you were meant to play in God's epic plan.

Don't Waste Your Life by John Piper. It's easy to slip through life without taking any risks and without making your life count, but life ought not be wasted. You don't need to know a lot of things to make a lasting difference in the world, but you do have to know the few, great, unchanging, and glorious things that matter and be willing to live and to die for them.

Start building your library of mission books to equip yourself to think and mobilize well! For the complete list of the top twenty-five books every mission mobilizer needs to read, scan the QR code.

99 View Support Raising as Mobilization.

Going short term or going long term? The odds are you will need to raise support. There are a lot of preconceived notions people have about support raising. People may feel like they are begging for money (not true); or they may feel they are settling by not working a "real" job. They may feel shame in asking people to give them money. What if we thought about support raising differently? What if we thought about support raising as an opportunity to mobilize our friends, family, churches, and acquaintances?

Support raising is a strategic process where you connect with people to share your passion for the world and why you are worthy of investment to engage with God's mission. Support raising is not a burden to bear so that you can do the good work of "going," it is a blessing that enables you to be a mobilizer while you invite other people to be senders. See your support raising season as a time to mobilize those you connect with for support.

100 Go to the I.T. Project.

Each summer The Traveling Team hosts the I.T. Project (Intensive Training Project). Students are invited to Los Angeles, CA. for seven weeks to go through an in-depth study of missions. Students spend the summer listening to missions' speakers from all over the world as well as visiting temples and mosques to get face-to-face with the world's major religions. Missionaries working in each of these religious groups come and equip students with evangelistic tools. Mission agencies to each major region and religion also come and share with the students.

At the I.T. Project, you will interact with Hare Krishna's, converse with the Imam at a mosque, listen to a devotee at the Buddhist temple, meet seasoned missionaries to the tribal world and get connected to people and opportunities abroad. Students are not only impacted, but are equipped with the practical information they need to follow through with their next steps!

The last week of the I.T. Project is designed to prepare students to go back to campus. Students make plans to implement world vision on their campus and in their campus ministries. The student who attends the I.T. Project not only goes deeper on a personal level, but is ready to mobilize other Christians to be World Christians. Consider giving a summer and to be trained at the I.T. Project. For more information, scan the QR code.

MOBILIZATION MATTERS

A good mobilizer helps others take steps of obedience in the mission, but a great mobilizer helps others understand "why" we should engage the mission. If we are to grow as mobilizers, we must model ourselves after the Master Mobilizer: Jesus.

Jesus is the master mobilizer because He always communicated His heart and purpose when asking His disciples to join His mission. In passages like Matthew 28:19-20, Luke 24:46-47, and John 20:21 we see that Jesus invites his friends to play a part in the mission, after He tells them of His authority over all things and the work of the Father. This is because mobilization, done correctly, always has a focus on Jesus and not simply the task at hand.

We would be wise to do the same in our mobilization! Not only should we encourage our friends to do tasks like download the "unreached of the day" app, but also share the heart behind why we pray for the world. Mobilization without vision will return void. We want to be great mobilizers who cast vision for the mission and not just next steps.

Jesus is worthy to be worshiped among every tribe, tongue, and nation—that is why we mobilize! We do not mobilize because God's mission seems to be a better life purpose for some people. We mobilize because Jesus is the only worthy one of all our attention, affection, and worship.

What does the Bible teach us about mobilization?

Read the following passages and make observations:

Nehemiah 2:1-8

Acts 11:1-18

Romans 15:24-28

Luke 24:45-48

2 Corinthians 5:17-20

Habakkuk 2:2

Ezekiel 33

Ezekiel 34

What is your greatest obstacle to mobilization?

_____

_____

_____

Think through all 25 ways to mobilize and pick one way you will mobilize this month.

_____

_____

_____

Who is someone who has mobilized you to God's mission? Write them a thank you card this week sharing how God used them to grow your vision for the world.

_____

_____

_____

Who is one friend you can mobilize with the World Vision Illustration? If you are unfamiliar with the illustration, watch the "how to video". (You can find the link in #76)

_____

_____

_____

101

WAYS TO GO

On May 25, 1961, John F. Kennedy addressed the United States Congress on "Urgent National Needs" and declared:

"I believe that this nation should commit itself to achieving the goal, before this decade [1960s] is out, of landing a man on the Moon and returning him safely to the Earth. No single space project in this period will be more impressive to mankind, or more important for the long-range exploration of space; and none will be so difficult or expensive to accomplish... [And] in a very real sense, it will not be one man going to the Moon—if we make this judgment affirmatively, it will be an entire nation. For all of us must work to put him there."

On July 16th, 1969 Apollo 11 launched from Cape Kennedy. Nearly a decade had disappeared between the day Kennedy made his declaration to the determined hour of launch. One can only imagine the many interruptions to travel plans that spanned nearly a decade of work. However, the task demanded constantly pushing the envelope. There were workers to be trained, tests to be run, strategies to stage, money to be allocated, losses to learn from, creativity to be fostered, and pivots to enact.

Along the journey there were 100's of ways to make impact in the mission. The space race was the culmination of over 25 billion dollars, the skills and dedication of nearly 300,000 technicians, and the solemn but certainly risk filled pledge of a president. A faint echo compared to Jesus' pledge and the labor of the church over the pages of history.

And yet, for all that impact and effort, one thing remained. In the end, the mission still demanded that three men climb aboard the space shuttle and 'Go!' No previous activity would substitute for this necessity. The waiting was over! This moon-landing mission required that men 'go!' No substitute could mitigate this demand. This reality was unmistakable among all who understood the task.

We too have been addressed on "Urgent Eternal Needs," by the King of Kings and Lord of Lords Himself, Jesus Christ. Jesus declared, "Go, therefore and make disciples of all nations!" (Matthew 28:19).

101 Go Overseas.

At the end of the day, we want to challenge you to go. Go for a summer and pray about a lifetime. If we want to see the world reached, we need people to go.

Greg and Sarah* were your average college students (*names changed for security purposes). They attended a well-known university and worked towards solid degrees like every other student. But something rocked their world and changed their plans.

They attended a summer training program where they learned about God's mission to reach the world, unreached peoples, praying for the nations, and welcoming international students. God used this summer to further grow their heart for God's mission, and to knit their own hearts closer together.

Greg and Sarah ended up getting married, and once they graduated, they desired to serve in a ministry that strategically welcomed international students on their campus. They did not see this as a long-term plan, but it was a time for development because they desired to see if the Lord would have them go. After serving with this ministry for a year, they connected with a mission agency that they wanted to go with, but knew they needed more development, and a healthy local church to be sent long-term. They worked as mobilizers for this organization for three years with their sights set on going long-term to the Muslim world.

After years of being patient, and getting the appropriate training, Greg and Sarah took a vision trip overseas to Central Asia, to see where the Lord would have them serve. They came back from this trip, and prayerfully decided on where the Lord would have them.

Today, they are in the final stages of preparation to go long-term to central Asia. Their goal is to faithfully serve overseas, among unreached people, for as long as the Lord will allow them.

When Greg and Sarah began growing their heart for the world, they did not know where they would end up long term, but they knew they wanted to take obedient steps of faith, out of their love for God, every step along the way. What would it look like for you to take a step of faith this year or this summer?

We recognize that you may not know how to go. A great place to start is MissionAgency.org. Scan the QR code and let The Traveling Team help you!

GO MAKE DISCIPLES

Someone had to board the shuttle to step onto the moon, and someone will have to board a plane to step into the unreached. The journey will be long. It will likely demand from you, that which you never expected. It may require a long-term address change. You can be certain that you will be personally changed! If not you, then who? And remember you don't go alone... You could change two words of the John F. Kennedy quote to read,

"But in a very real sense, it will not be one man going to the nations—if we make this judgment affirmatively, it will be the entire church. For all must work to put him there."

What does the Bible teach us about going?

Read the following passages and make observations:

Matthew 28:18-20

Mark 16:15

Luke 24:47

John 20:21

Acts 1:8

Romans 15:20

Romans 10:14-15

What is your greatest obstacle to going?

_____

_____

_____

Is there a place in the world where you want to go?

_____

_____

_____

Visit The Traveling Team's website to find credible mission agencies. Write down three agencies you want to learn more about. You can fill out www.missionagency.org and staff from The Traveling Team can discuss next steps.

_____

_____

_____

Who is one friend you can mobilize to go with you on an overseas trip?

_____

_____

_____

DON'T WASTE YOUR WAITING

There we have it —101 ways to impact the world even when you experience obstacles to going overseas. The aim in creating this list was not to overwhelm, but to inspire us to dig a little deeper to play a part in the mission of God.

What if God is beckoning us to open our eyes and see that the very fabric of how we live our lives needs to change? Maybe God wants us to see that as important as going is to fulfill His mission; praying, welcoming, giving and mobilizing are equally vital. As stated, we absolutely need to go. We need long-term, cross-cultural workers who hear the call of God in scripture and move to the unreached. We need to continue to go on short-term trips. But we also absolutely need faithful prayers, givers, welcomers, and mobilizers. Just as it is sacrificial to pick up your life and move across the globe, the way we give, pray, welcome, and mobilize should be no less sacrificial.

THE GLORY OF GOD TO ALL NATIONS

You have a unique and profound opportunity to engage in all 101.

We do not want you to miss it. We do not want you to miss being a part of the greatest story ever told, stepping into the mission of God, because the idea we have of missions is limited to a summer trip.

You were born to be in relationship with your Heavenly Father and live your life according to His Word. God's Word clearly shows us that He has sovereignly and lovingly invited his children, you, and me, to play a role in seeing the Great Commission fulfilled! I cannot conjure up a higher calling for our lives. How that plays out for each of us will look different, as God has gifted us with different skills and passions, but the root remains the same: the glory of God made known in all nations. Does God need our help? No! But He delights in bringing us into the story and using us as conduits of His grace to reach all peoples on earth.

Revelation 7:9 says, "After this I looked, and behold, a great multitude that no one could number, from every nation, from all tribes and peoples and languages, standing before the throne and before the Lamb...." This is a future picture of heaven. God's mission complete. All of history is headed to and culminates here, and we can be a part of seeing that happen.

We want you to go when you can go, but when that is not an option, let's keep an eternal perspective and make the most of the abundance of opportunity God has placed before us. It may require a deeper level of intentionality, but our prayer is that these 101 ways move you towards the heart of God and spurs you to action with a passion to see the gospel reach the ends of the Earth.

IS THERE MORE TO MISSIONS THAN GOING?

When it comes to missions, our lens is often too narrow. We limit playing a role in God's mission to going overseas, when that is simply one way to see the world reached. This book will give you practical ways on how to engage in God's global mission. We will walk you through 101 different ways to engage in God's mission right now. These tangible acts will lead to the cultivation of global Christian habits and obedience while growing your heart for God and His world.

We do not want you to miss being part of the greatest story ever told, stepping into the mission of God, because the idea we have of missions is limited to a summer trip. You have a unique and profound opportunity to engage in all 101 ways.

Your role may not involve a cross-cultural move, but it will always involve a cross-carrying sacrifice.

This resource was produced by The Traveling Team. The Traveling Team exists to mobilize Christian university students across the country to become global Christians who engage in World Evangelization. We travel campus to campus, share a Biblical basis of missions, and help students find their role as goers and senders. We hope this book impacts you and inspires you to find your role in God's global mission.

THE
TRAVELING
TEAM

ISBN 978-0-578-85043-6

9 780578 850436

90000

:camera: THETRAVELINGTEAM | :f: THETRAVELINGTEAM

WWW.THETRAVELINGTEAM.ORG

CPSIA information can be obtained
at www.ICGtesting.com
Printed in the USA
LVHW060100240721
693230LV00001BC/2

9 780578 850436